STUDENT ENTREPRENEURS

A Handbook on How to Catch Them Young

DEEPA UNNITHAN

HAREESH N RAMANATHAN

INDIA • SINGAPORE • MALAYSIA

Book's Objective

This book is an attempt to present and consider student entrepreneurs as a distinct genus with their competencies, temperaments and motivations vastly different from the defined expectations of a traditional entrepreneur. The dreamy eyed youngsters inspired by the glorious stories of entrepreneurial success and lenient seed funding schemes tend to overlook the realistic scenario of business formation, resulting in premature shutdown. The key objective of the book is to encourage aspiring students to take a learnt decision on their entrepreneurial future weighing the pros and cons of personal self and the operating socio-economic environmental framework through validated instruments. The book will enable startup mentors with a toolkit to screen their students on their realistic potential so that need based support can be provided to grow the promising one while diverting others to more suitable career options.

Contents

Acknowledgement

I pay my obeisance to Lord Balaji, for the blessings bestowed upon me for the completion of this book and always.

With profound gratitude, I acknowledge the guidance of Prof. (Dr.) Hareesh N Ramanathan, my co-author, who has been a real mentor and role model. I shall be eternally thankful to him for his continuous persuasion which made this book possible.

I am indebted to Dr. Francisco Liñán, Full Professor (Catedrático) at Universidad de Sevilla, Spain for sharing the scales and references which guided the research needed for this book.

I thank CA Venugopal C Govind, Chairman-Bharatiya Vidya Bhavan for his keen interest in the academic human capital and Prof. (Dr.) Rajagopala Nair, Dean, Bhavan's B-School for always giving the "go ahead" for my plans and proposals.

I express my sincere gratitude to the Principals, Department Heads and students of various colleges for rendering help for my survey to validate the tools used in the book.

A special word of thanks to Ms.Jayasri Rajan, for the library support and encouragement.

Many thanks to Notionpress team for your seamless and efficient support in the publishing process.

Words cannot express my deep obligation to my beloved mother, father and dearest husband –epitomes of unconditional positive regard, for being my driving force instilling courage in all my difficult moments, and for all your sacrifices for me. The love and understanding shown by my little son and daughter was immeasurable. I also thank my in-laws for their moral support.

I wish to dedicate this book at the lotus feet of Lord Balaji.

– Deepa Unnithan

I would like to thank all my friends, colleagues and entrepreneurs who have provided advice and feedback in the pursuit of being an entrepreneur mentor. From casual tea conversations to lengthy brainstorming, your inputs were much essential. Special thanks to Each of the students who participated in our surveys that enabled us to gain insights about the content of this book. Our gratitude to the people in the entrepreneurship ecosystem who agreed to provide an interview.

While the research for this book was going on helped to shape and bring the book personal insights from a variety of perspectives. Many thanks to each of you. As you all are extremely busy and talented people, your time and candor in our discussions were a great gift.

I appreciate the time and effort put for the preparation and reading of the manuscript by the co author Dr Deepa Unnithan.

A special note of thanks goes to my family, friends from the academic fraternity.

Thank you as well to Notionpress for the editorial and production staff who were encouraging as well as skillful in finalizing the publication in every aspect.

– Hareesh N Ramanathan

Preface

Everyone talks about entrepreneurship as the most happening phenomenon of the era. Startups are considered as the panacea for sluggish employment conditions in many of the countries. Policy makers leave no stone unturned for the development of entrepreneurs who are the job creators for a self-reliant economy. More and more research to catch them as young as possible and nurturing them with sufficient ecosystem support is a quintessential objective of government around the world. The massive success of student developed models which later turned to be global conglomerates namely Google, Microsoft, Facebook and the like has created an upsurge in the entrepreneurial aspirations of students. The perspective towards self-employment as a risky narrow road for the adventurous only has been shifted to an easy well laid career path towards success and glory for youngsters from campuses.

Inspired by the success stories of the iconic startups, and motivated by the environmental support, students give wings to their entrepreneurial dreams through setting up a startup right from their campus itself. But will that flourish or perish is a matter of concern as only a few of the startups by student founders scale up or get acquired despite availing all kinds of mentoring and financing. Should the policy initiatives reach its ambitious goals, a pragmatic and realistic approach is needed to convert a reasonable percentage of students' startup ideas to revenue generating business entities. The first step in this direction is differentiating student entrepreneurs, who are young and naïve. The patterns and methods of entrepreneurial development used in traditional entrepreneurship requires modifications as approaches towards formation of student entrepreneurs need to address not only their potential but their inexperience, excitement and anxieties too. Further, there is a need to realistically assess the actual potential of the student and the generated idea to scale up within the prevailing socio-economic environmental framework.

This book is an attempt to characterise student entrepreneurs and their business formation pattern through a methodical approach. It provides a set of scientific tools and explanations which the reader can use to assess the characteristics of a student as a potential entrepreneur and thereby making the crucial decision; to follow the entrepreneurial pursuit or not.

Chapter 1

Student Entrepreneur-the New Genus

"If you want something new, you have to stop doing something old."

– Peter Drucker

Naughty Boy in College to Poster Boy for Entrepreneurship

"Facemash creator survives Adboard", read the headline of Harvard Crimson, November 19, 2003, the daily newspaper of Harvard. The story is about the disciplinary action against Mark Zuckerberg, a second-year student who narrowly escaped expulsion for developing a popular site to rank student photos based on "hot or not" (The Harvard Crimson 2003). Based on a friend's idea, the young boy was fascinated to work on programming and algorithm for a product that could kill boredom in the university dorm. He faced punishment from university administration for objectifying students and had to withdraw Facemash within two weeks of its launch to drop the charges. He iterated the concept as a study tool for comparison and notes sharing on art history, which was well accepted by the student and teachers. Later on, Zuckerberg developed a centralised website which served as an online directory for all Harvard members and connected people around the university. With an initial investment of 2000 dollars, half of it by his friend Eduard, the site got launched on February 4, 2004 under the name of "The Facebook". Later in an article published in the flagship Harvard Business Review, May 18, 2012 mentions Zuckerberg like this," he is a role model for a generation whose members view entrepreneurship as the best avenue to express themselves and serve society with their work".

1.1 Students are the Future-In Entrepreneurship too

So, you have picked up this book either because you are a student interested to be an entrepreneur or you are someone interested to help students to be entrepreneurs. Today's students are tomorrow's value creators in all spheres of existence, let alone entrepreneurship, the key to sustenance in an uncertain future. World around, the initial buzz created by the student businesses has subdued for appreciating the grander milieu allied to the same. In addition to the student fraternity and policymakers, society at large has realised the ever increasing scope of students turning entrepreneurs. The harsh truth that well-established firms may not generate a net increase in employment was realised by western nations in the 1970s itself. In countries like India, the pace at which startup unicorns emerge itself within positive ecosystems indicates how entrepreneurial spirit among youth is critical to the need for societies' achievement of economic development. This has put forth a new turn of events which reflected a growing interest tacit as the generation of novel independent entrepreneurship[1] by youngsters who mostly are first generation entrepreneurs. This newfound interest in entrepreneurship captured the attention, furthermore instilled a positive image of entrepreneurship as a career option among students[2] and

1 (Davidsson 1995)

2 (Henderson 1999)

the possibilities of triggering and creating small business owners.

The significance of promoting entrepreneurial sparks of students cannot be overemphasised. These stakeholders of tomorrow's world could be converted from job seekers to job creators, as the motto always goes. But for that, the first step is to know who is a student entrepreneur. Handpicking the right one from the crowd of dreamy eyed lot from the schools and colleges for early orientation on the path ahead in a realistic note will help to mould a healthy entrepreneurial economy, not a graveyard of student startups.

The Bansals, Sachin and Binny who cofounded the one of India's earliest startups, Flipkart, met at the IIT lab as they both were stuck in the campus during the summer vacation due to the non-submission of their summer projects. Their friendship grew and they moved together to ecommerce giant Amazon as engineers, where they realised each other's soul searching was to start something new. In no time they quit Amazon and with a pooled investment of 4 lakhs and lot of passion, they redefined the ecommerce platform in India through Flipkart.

Findings on the direct causal relationship between the students' business orientations and regional economic growth were conclusively reported in several parts of the world based on panel studies. A study on university students in Turkey threw light to strong entrepreneurial orientation among students which could bloom if contextual support is available[3]. Greek students found to have positive perceptions of starting a business during their university days or in future[4]. Nigerian Universities concluded that the region's economic growth could be boosted through inculcating self-employment and business entrepreneurship among students[5]. Direct relationship between startup growth and employment growth were reported from Sweden[6]. In Portugal, studies showed that students are motivated to start their own business ventures right after graduation[7]. Meantime MITs, Bostons and Harvards had evolved as temples of student entrepreneurship. All these point to the fact that the intensity of entrepreneurial attitude is quite high in the minds of students and appreciating these forces which contribute to the birth of student entrepreneurship is extremely crucial.

Consensus on the perspective that student entrepreneurship is a panacea for poverty, employment growth and vehicle for change in the regional industry is widely shared, as every percentage point rise in entrepreneurship is directly proportional to a two per cent fall rate of poverty[8]. The tremendous impact on societal welfare that can be brought in by the drive of student entrepreneurship is very significant.

---

3 (Atsan 2006)

4 (Apergis and Fafaliou 2011)

5 (Agbim 2013)

6 (Andersson and Noseleit 2009)

7 (Gerry, Marques and Noguei 2008)

8 (Fisher and Duane 2016)

Though the spirit of student entrepreneurship has been well acknowledged as the most potent source of innovation, there are grey areas as to the fine knowledge on the differential treatment needed for them from the traditional entrepreneurship models. A "one size fits all" entrepreneurial development method will not be effective, as these budding entrepreneurs are a community of young and naïve' dreamers passionate with an idea but inexperienced about the realistic journey of commercial venture creation.

1.2 Traditional Entrepreneurship Vs Student Entrepreneurship

It's really a matter of concern whether conventional definitions of entrepreneurship and entrepreneur suit the present phenomenon of student entrepreneurship. Early economists defined entrepreneurship as speculation in search of profit in uncertain circumstances[9] and as the process of innovation creating disequilibrium to achieve progress thus making the entrepreneur an innovator[10]. Entrepreneurs are believed to possess the behavioural traits such as self-confident, goal-oriented, moderated risk-taker, creative, proactive, risk-taking, innovative ability in the pursuit of opportunity not considering the resource constraints. Entrepreneurial activity is often interpreted as resourceful human action in quest of the value generation, by way of formation of or expansion

9 (Cantillon 1931)

10 (Schumpeter 1942)

of economic activity, by identifying and developing new products, processes or markets. Entrepreneurship could be explained as the phenomena concomitant with this entrepreneurial action[11]. Over the years, more wholesome definitions mentioning the process, person and effects of creating opportunities for future came up.

Furthermore, considering the flexible nature of entrepreneurship, its each dimension influences other, making the entrepreneur's personal traits and venture features inseparable, highlighting the management pattern. Management thinkers attribute features like business innovation, new business creation, innovation, opportunity seeking, risk assumption, top management teams and group processes in strategic decisions. Modern researchers try to segregate corporate entrepreneurship as an strategic advanced level whereas start-up entrepreneurship as primary entry level business[12]. Despite all these, a concrete definition of entrepreneurship is hard to put forth as it implies different salience to different streams. A conceptual comparison of different schools of thoughts on the definition of conventional entrepreneurship mapped in the illustration, in **Fig No.2.2.**

11 (Ahmad and Seymour 2008)

12 (Sciascia and De Vita 2014)

Economist's Approach	Behavioral Approach	Management Approach
• Cantillon, 1931 • (Profit Seeking Activity) • Schumpeter, 1936 • (Innovation) • Kirzner, 1973 • (Exploitation of Opportunities) • Ahmad&Seymour, 2008 • (Value Generation through Economic Activity)	• Timmons, 1978 • (Proactivemess, Risk Taking, Innovative Ability) • Cauthorn, 1989 • (Self Confidence, Goal Orientation, Risk Taking, Creativity) • Stevenson&Jarillo, 1990 • (Opportunity Seeking)	• Peter Drucker, 1985 • (Business Innovation) • Sandberg, 1992 • (New business creation, innovation, risk assumption, strategic decisions through group processes) • Morris&Kuratko, 2002 • (Managerial Style) • Synskey&Yonekura, 2002 • (Flexible& Interdependent)

Fig No.2.2 Conventional Entrepreneurship Definitions- Conceptual Comparison

The extent to which definitions of conventional entrepreneurship as an economic activity of profit and value generation by people of identified behavioural traits and management competency are explanatory enough for the concept of student entreprenurship is debatable. The dimensions of entreprenurship are multiple and inter dependable; the expectations of conventional entrepreneurship might be congruent with student entrepreneurs also in varying extent. Nevertheless, the ideal approach would be to segregate student entrepreneurship as young and basic entry-level startup concept different from strategic corporate entrepreneurship. This approach is justified based on the rationale that many of the student businesses in the fast forward contemporary world thrive on the revolutionary concept of agile innovation wherein projects are swiftly built around motivated youngsters, if proper support system is in place. This is so characteristic of almost all student entrepreneurial ecosystem, especially with technology-based incubates commonly seen in almost all higher educational institutions.

Manik Gupta and his roommate Pradeep Kumar, both 3rd year law students at AIL Mohali were doing their practical assignments on basic legal drafting using real life client projects. With semester exams months away, they planned to put their newly learned skill to practical business offering a legal service platform Lawin1, a name created instantly from an all-in-one snack box packet which they spotted on their hostel floor. In no time, these student entrepreneurs could branch out their venture with growing client base as well as reputation, and before their final exams, Lawin1 got acquired for a whopping $5,84,000.

Traditional entrepreneurship models are typically causal in nature wherein the ultimate outcome is foreseen well in advance. But most of the successful student businesses have sprung out of hostel rooms with less or no capital, pointing towards an effectual model where business is started within given means and seek to create new ends using non-predictive strategies[13]. This overlaps with the profile of the interns in business incubators,

13 (Sarasvathy 2003)

as they have started operating on their business ideas from classrooms without fretting about the future uncertainties[14]. While the traditional entrepreneurships were considered as solutions for achieving value generation through economic activity and business innovation, the new age student business focus on innovation through design thinking where preconceived problem definitions are not very important, but new equations and paths are undertaken to reach the goals of innovation[15]. Moreover, rather than producing goods and services for an identified market, the student business owners tend to follow an imagination driven expeditionary marketing[16] where new markets are created and customers are lead to them, much with the support of IoT. Another essential aspect that is to be added to the specific attribute of student start-ups is the lean nature of management against the hierarchical personnel intensive old entrepreneurship models. Students start their business singly or mostly in association with their like-minded close friends once they are ready to fly out after mentoring and incubation rather than pursuing a large scale business launch. The broad comparison of explicit features of traditional entrepreneurship and student entrepreneurship has been presented in Table 2.1

---

14 (Ramanathan and Unnithan 2015)

15 (Fisher and Duane 2016)

16 (Prahlad 1991)

Criteria	Traditional Entrepreneurship	Student Entrepreneurship
Decision Making	Any time	During Student Life
Innovation	Market-driven	Idea Driven
Business Model	Causal	Effectual
Business Development	Structured based on Problem	Agile based on Design
Management Style	People Intensive	Lean

Table 2.1 Feature-based Comparison of Traditional Entrepreneurship and Student Entrepreneurship

1.3 Student Entrepreneurship-Definition

It's good to define student entrepreneurship encompassing all its characteristic peculiarities to create awareness as well as work upon this concept in a distinguished manner from traditional entrepreneurial models.

Student entrepreneur is one who has identified or realised entrepreneurial spark during studentship itself and decided to pursue entrepreneurship parallel or immediately after the course by actively seeking guidance and support for nurturing entrepreneurial intentions during studentship and consistently stick to entrepreneurship as livelihood despite uncertain environmental factors. Student entrepreneurship is the enterprise resulting from the intense entrepreneurial intention of a student entrepreneur.

So, ask yourself whether these characteristics speak of you. Or if you are a mentor, spot that student with these characteristics.

- Innovative and Enterprising in the campus
- Unperturbed by Challenges
- Starts the venture in parallel with the course or immediately after
- Actively seeking guidance and support

Early identification of entrepreneurial spark right at the time of being a student is a necessary aspect. This could be self-realisation of one's enterprising abilities or being spotted by someone else during life as a student in the school or college through the innovatively distinct ideas and methods. The student would have embarked on its entrepreneurial journey from the campus itself if she gets an avenue to pursue the same while doing the course either as a business owner in the free time or make use of the institution support to do business as part of the course itself. However, those students who realised their aptitude though decided to finish the course first and later commence the entrepreneurial venture also come under the category of student entrepreneurs as the initial spark has been identified at this stage.

The twelve-year-old, Shubham Banerjee stumbled upon the need for affordable braille materials during a quick research for his science fair project. With his Lego Mindstorm robotics play kit and hours of repeated attempts, he created Braigo, an inexpensive and unique braille printer, which made him not only the winner in the science fair, but the founder of "Braigo labs" by the time he turned 13, the venture capital backed firm with patented products to help the blind, with his mom as the President and dad as the advisor. With permission from his school, he attends conferences, make keynote deliveries and continuously look for making innovations.

The students who have made up their minds are less apprehensive and unreserved to seek active guidance and support while comparing to the traditional businessmen may be due to the young age and curiosity. Once they have identified their passion, the students are willing to go any extent to create networks, nowadays catalysed by the social media advantages, to explore, seek guidance and opportunities to showcase their ideas so that their dreams get wings and they will be able to fly. Moreover, they are unperturbed by the challenges that may come across either as low examination grades, sceptic family, economic uncertainties and the like as they are naïve and the entrepreneurship concept they have conceived is dearer to them emotionally than the practicalities around it. This makes them more perseverant and hardworking towards their goal which eventually makes them self-employed and earning them their livelihood.

The business model developed by a student which gets converted to an enterprise either at the campus or outside can be considered as student entrepreneurship.

Are you a student entrepreneur?

Here is a self assessment exercise for you to check your entrepreneurial interest as a student.

Mark your responses to the statements based on your level of agreement with the following statements, indicating 5-Very much true; 4-Somewhat true; 3-Not sure/May be; 2 –Somewhat Untrue 1-Very Untrue

1. *I think entrepreneurship is right for me.*
2. *I have been seriously considering entrepreneurship as a career choice even while in school or college.*
3. *I can work upon my business idea along with my studies or immediately after the course.*
4. *I have a clear plan about what am I going to do with my business idea.*
5. *I have discussed my entrepreneurship plans with others.*
6. *I participate in programmes and events to understand more about entrepreneurship.*
7. *I am working on a network to create a support system for my entrepreneurship.*
8. *I am able to manage any challenge in my entrepreneurial path.*
9. *I actively seek guidance from any possible source to pursue my entrepreneurial dreams.*
10. *I closely follow the market developments in my area of interest.*

Find your total score and compare it with the standards below.

- If the score is more than 40, you are in the right direction to be a student entrepreneur, keep it up!

- If the score is in the range of 30-40, you need to be some more focused with your student entrepreneurship, try harder!
- If the score is less than 30, you may not be a student entrepreneur, sometimes a traditional entrepreneurship option may be suitable, think over!

In a validation exercise conducted among a group of 500 students from different backgrounds 17% scored more than 40, while 56% scored in the range of 30-45 points and 27% scored less than 30 points.

Got an Idea? An Easy Formula to Convert an Idea to Entrepreneurial Opportunity

Now that you have recognised yourself as a student entrepreneur in the making, let us look at how that spectacular seed idea of yours could be grown into an entrepreneurial opportunity. A good idea is a springboard of any entrepreneurial aspirant. It could be in terms of breakthrough innovation as an idea for a new market offering, a new process of doing things, a new method of delivery, a new unserved market and so on which serves to address any pain point existing in the market. Thus an idea will become a solution to resolve any problem or need gaps which the pre-existing products or services could not satisfy thereby adding value to those who are willing to spend on it. Developing a solid business model devised around the value proposition through the identification of resources, strategies, cost structure and revenue streams will enable to operationalise the idea into a viable entrepreneurial opportunity. This model of converting a seed idea to an opportunity could be understood as an easy formula presented as an equation below.

Infographic on Entrepreneurial Opportunity Equation

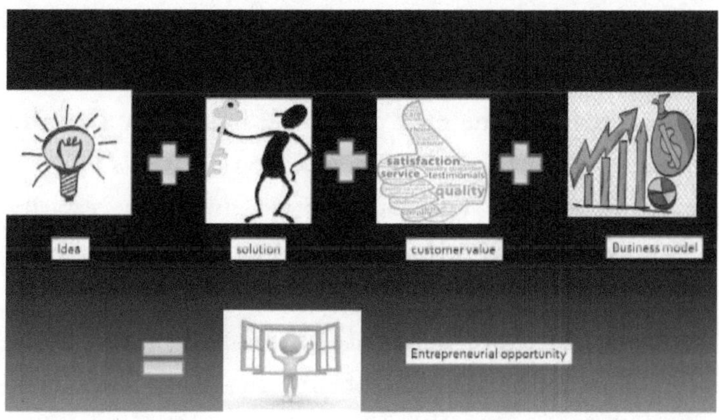

Students are storehouses of creative ideas nurtured and showcased through manifold opportunities available to them and academic institutions. Creativity challenges, innovation hunts, business plan contests etc. are regular in schools and colleges today. Despite being great ideas with business potential as well as ecosystem support, only a very less percentage of them get converted to entrepreneurship. After the initial excitement and euphoria of winning and appreciation, most students tend to be complacent to pursue the ideas with needed efforts and perseverance. Those students who feel the entrepreneurial spark from within to process the idea to a value-adding concept decide to build a business model, facing any difficulty with passion. They will eventually come out as student entrepreneurs who carve their future themselves.

No Idea? Let's Search

If you feel you could have nailed it, but deprived of an idea to start –don't worry, there are plenty of options which you could explore to source an idea from. The key thing is to train the eyes to see the unseen gaps in the markets so that the brain can give you ideas as solutions to fill these gaps. These ideas need not be necessarily unique, can be exceptional execution of the existing ones too. It can spring from modifications of an otherwise regular product for a better use, introducing automation, simplification or convenience to the user, your own personal interests or hobbies, work experiences, skills, abilities –think expansively without any boundaries, judgements and assumptions.

Mentors can guide students to generate ideas through proven idea generation techniques like brainstorming, lateral thinking, mind mapping, SCAMPER, Gordon method, attribute listing, morphological analysis, synectics, free association, forced relationships, big dream method, collective notebook etc. These conventional idea generation techniques which are widely used in encouraging creative thinking and generating out of the box ideas. Vetting the ideas by experts through a stop error method or Real-Win-Win (RWW) could ensure students to weed out the unviable ones early on and pursue only the promising idea channelizing the time, energy and aspirations.

Opportunity Recognition Analysis

An opportunity is the bridge between the idea and the customer pain point. The idea, how much ever it sounds promising, should be subjected to a thorough pre-analysis with respect to its potential to get converted to a profitable opportunity which can add value to customer lives. It should be well aligned with the underlying market needs and wants, the personal competencies of the entrepreneur for sustained value delivery as well as driven by passion and commitment. The recognition of opportunity is the pivoting point in deciding the fate of the business idea which transforming it into an innovation. Students should attempt to develop a business model addressing the need gap identified in the market to verify the idea as a viable business opportunity. Tools like lean canvas template, concept boards etc. can help the students to translate their business idea into strategic business model while evaluating all the key elements of the opportunity.

The opportunity recognition analysis need to be done with a strong focus on the market as well as the aspiring students' strengths and weaknesses. The mentors can help the students to showcase their idea and validate it using a lean canvas method, concept boards, or any other method which enable the student to map and visusalise the idea around the need gaps identified, how the business idea could be a solution to the address the need gap evaluating the expected cashflows, investments, strategies as well as value delivery model. Refining the business model with continuous research and discussions will help the student to have a holistic view of his entrepreneurial opportunity well in advance.

Steve Jobs, the most iconic innovator in startup world, is known for his creativity and out of box methods which made him always thinking about doing things in new ways thus leading to amazing solutions through Apple. Harland David Sanders, aka Colonel Sanders created the finger licking good recipe for his Kentucky Fried Chicken in his perseverant trial to cook chicken faster in a pressure fryer. A short stint as a trainee in a biopharmaceutical company made Kiran Mazumdar Shaw, who always wanted to be a master brewer in her young age, to set up Biocon fighting against all odds of an unconventional businessmodel, youth and gender at a tender age of 25 converting it to a biopharmaceutical giant and still pursuing opportunities for affordable innovation. Jeff Bezoz has never stopped asking more and more questions and seeking answers finding new and new opportunities to grow the mighty Amazon. When Anita Roddick thought about setting up a cosmetics venture for distributing natural cosmetics in the name Body Shop, that shaped a new movement called ethical consumerism. The enchanting beauty Priyanka Chopra is one who has a penchant for continuous opportunity recognition, let that be her Miss Universe title, striking film roles or entrepreneurial partnerships through Bumble bee dating app, foodpreneurship through Sona restaurant or natural hair care through Anomaly brand.

Purposeful innovation should evolve through systematic opportunity recognition analysis. It needs a focused approach in a consistent manner which is more of work than genius. Continuous innovations through continuous opportunity recognitions serve the foundation of entrepreneurship. Just relax and keep your eyes and minds open, you will spot an opportunity around you. Flip to the next pages to check whether you are cut to pursue the opportunity to a full-fledged venture.

Chapter 2

The Entrepreneurial Spark-Intention

At twenty, if you are not an idealist, then you don't have a heart. And if you continue being an idealist at forty, then you don't have a brain."

– Sudha Murty

Ironman to Robot Scavenger- The Bandicoot Story

Just like most other kids of their age, Vimal Govind and friends were also fascinated with Ironman and robotics. During their engineering college days, developing an Ironman exoskeleton as an academic project got them good grades and a lot of appreciation. Inspired by this, they planned to set up a hardware startup and named it "Genrobotics". Though, due to the lack of finance and other commitments they had to forego the entrepreneurial dreams and landed up in secured jobs through campus placements. In 2015, an incident reported in newspapers- three people died in the process of manual scavenging after being stuck in a manhole for 30 minutes. This happened in their native place Kerala, and was a real moment of revelation on the lack of any engineering products to replace manual scavenging. Backed up by their engineering skills and handholding by Kerala Startup Mission, the twentysomethings quit their jobs to their parents' dismay, to come up with a solution. In 2018, after a lot of research and groundwork supported by the Kerala Government, Bandicoot, the scavenging robot was unveiled. It was consciously developed in a way that need to be operated by the same scavenging workforce to ensure that the existing labourers do no lose their jobs. This technology to save human lives got wide recognition, and what started as an apprehensive student entrepreneurship has grown big as a thriving innovation model.

2.1 Feeling a Spark, Let's Find Out!

Do you feel a spark within on and often to do something hands-on to live your life? A strong passion to be your master and make a change in others' life as well?Yes, that would be the buzzing "entrepreneurial intention" within you!! Intentionality for entrepreneurship is the closest measurable aspect which could be considered as a starting point for identifying the entrepreneurial spark among students. Early identification of the entrepreneurial spark and kindling that with necessary support is the key to the growth of student entrepreneurship.The entrepreneurial intention has been vibrant as a critical area of global discussion and research. It is considered as the initial strategic template of new organisations and essential underpinnings of new venture development[17]. This chapter will help you understand and conceptualise enterprenurial intention so that you could assess the strength of the spark you are feeling right now.

The formation of entrepreneurial intentions (EIs) is of critical interest as they are considered the best predictors of entrepreneurial behavior[18]. Intentions are assumed to capture the motivational factors that influence a behavior; they are indications of how hard people are willing to try, of how much of an effort they are planning to exert in order to perform the behavior. As a general rule, the

17 (Bird, 1988)

18 (Krueger & Brazeal, 1994)

stronger the intention to engage in a behavior, the more likely should be its performance[19].

As an individual, your intenton would be driven by various factors. It could be by the implicit desires like meaning and purpose of life or explicit aspirations like monetary reward. More favourable an individual is towards the thought of starting a new business venture; the more will be his entrepreneurial intention. Thus we can say that a good positive appraisal of entrepreneurship can translate to an intention to start something of your own. The focus on any kind of intention, irrespective of entrepreneurial or other, has long been studied based on individual behaviour and personal dispositions. Let us take a glimpse of different pieces of literatures which underlines the need to closely examine the intention for starting a new venture.

Literature	*Perspective*
(Bird, 1988)	EI is the initial strategic template of the new venture
(Ajzen I., 1991)	Intention captures motivation to any behaviour
(Krueger N. F., 2000)	EI reflects the founder's vision of an emerging organisation
(Kolvereid & Isaksen, 2006)	Measuring EI can predict venture creation and growth
(Liñán & Chen, 2006)	Internal cognitive mechanisms of EI are the same despite regional differences
(Wu J., 2009)	EI defines near future entrepreneurship

19 (Ajzen I., 1991)

(Franco M. H., 2010)	EI reasons individual's entrepreneurial career
(Rittippant & Kokchang, 2011)	EI examines both internal and external motivators of entrepreneurship
(Liñán, Cohard, & -Cantuche, 2011)	Last year students have empirically high EI
(Prabhu, McGuire, & Dros, 2012)	Manifestations of EI among youngsters- general, lifestyle, high growth.
(Mungai, 2013)	Regional differences affect EI
(Philipp Sieger, 2014)	Students' EI is of high interest among stakeholders
(Valliere, 2016)	EI is a personal conviction to exploit business opportunities

Table No 2.2 Key Perspectives on the Role of Entrepreneurial Intention for New Venture Creation

Going by these insights, if entrepreneurship is to be encouraged among a group, their entrepreneurial intentions need to be explored first as the initial strategic template. This applied to student communities as well. When proactive young men and women are highly confident about their belief in their entrepreneurial capabilities, they want to – and intend to – start businesses[20]. The opportunity identification process is intentional. Intentions refer to the target behaviour and even the culture of starting a business.

Much like Ritesh Agarwal, the founder of OYO, who identified a business opportunity in the" non-availability" of clean and affordable hotel rooms whil travelling. With

20 (Prabhu, McGuire, & Dros, 2012)

steady improvisation in the line of Airbnb, Oyo created a new travel culture in no time, all when he was just 19 years old.

The concept of EI is not free from criticisms. Researchers argue that EI is probably not a single construct. Students whose behaviour has not effectively generated any action makes it impossible to measure in terms of whether or not they have set up a company which poses a challenge to understand the implementation of entrepreneurial intention. However, in some cases, this intention is formed only shortly before the actual decision and in some other cases, the intention never leads to actual behaviour. Hence, entrepreneurial intentions are assumed to predict, although imperfectly, individuals' choice to found their firms[21]. While it is certainly possible to tap into what might be called "general EI," some variations should also be considered. Serious thoughts around Student's Entrepreneurial Intention(SEI) has started lately after certain first-generation businessmen have proven themselves in their studentship itself or have successfully commercialised their business ideas evolved during their student days. By corroborating these latest developments with the pre-existing theories of entrepreneurial intention would be apt to understand the dimensions in which the concept of EI unfolds.

21 (Davidsson P., 1995)

2.2 Theoretical Models of Entrepreneurial Intention

Let us discuss a little theory to figure out entrepreurial intentions.

Robust and parsimonious models of entrepreneurial intentions with considerable proven predictive value draw influences from social psychology as well as the comprehensive environment of entrepreneurship. Early researchers had formulated models which examined entrepreneurship as a very innate and endogenous socio-psychological behaviour which in turn has spillover influences from environmental attributes. However, recently researchers have come up with verifiable indicators on the role of exogenous environmental factors in configuring the entrepreneurial intention, especially among students.

Shapero's model of Entrepreneurial Event theory (SEE), is regarded as a fundamental model explaining entrepreneurial intentions. According to this theory, the entrepreneurial intention of an individual is decided on two aspects, namely perceived feasibility and perceived desirability[22]. By perceived desirability, degree of attraction an individual perceives towards a particular behaviour, like starting an entrepreneurial venture. Perceived feasibility refers to the perception regarding the self-capability to perform that particular behaviour. Another view is, intentionality is a state of mind directing a person's attention (therefore experience and action)

22 (Shapero & Sokol, 1982)

toward a specific objective (goal) or a path to achieve something (means). It is influenced by society, policy and economic changes, market as well as changes in control systems. Entrepreneurial intentions are aimed at either creating a new venture or creating new values in existing ventures. It is the entrepreneur's intention that guides him in the process of entrepreneurship[23]. This model evaluated entrepreneurial intention from an intrapsychic as well social organisation perspective.

In Davidsson's psychologic economic model, the primary determinant of entrepreneurial intention is a person's conviction that starting and running one's firm is a suitable alternative for him/her. This conviction is in its turn based on certain general attitudes and domain attitudes. The former refers to more general psychological dispositions whereas the latter specifically concern entrepreneurship and owner-managed firms.

Jeff Bezoz was always curious and inquisitive as a youngster. Though he was very confident about his own technological proficiencies and scientific interests, he had warned all his early investors a 70 % chance of Amazon would fail or go bankrupt. What started as an online bookstore went public with an Initial Public Offering, just in 3 years.

Theory of Planned behaviour, formulated by Ajzen, which is famously considered as the bottom rock of entrepreneurial intention, established that intentions

23 (Bird, 1988)

are assumed to capture the motivational factors that influence behaviour; they are indications of how hard people are willing to try, of how much of an effort they are planning to exert, to perform the behaviour. As a general rule, the stronger the intention to engage in a behaviour, the more likely should be its performance. The theory of planned behaviour (TPB) postulates three conceptually independent determinants of intention.[24]

- *Attitude toward the behaviour (ATB):* the degree to which a person has a favourable or unfavourable evaluation or appraisal of the behaviour in question.
- *Subjective norm (SN):* the perceived social pressure to perform or not to perform the behaviour.
- *Perceived behavioural control (PBC)*: the perceived ease or difficulty of performing the behaviour

In the purview of students' based studies, TPB focuses on situations in which an individual has incomplete volitional control, that is, on situations in which the individual cannot decide entirely at will whether to perform a certain behaviour or not. Instead, for the individual to perform the behaviour, she needs to exercise a sufficient degree of actual and perceived control over the behaviour itself and the outcome of the behaviour. TPB is applied to the study of individual behaviour and where there is a short time-lapse between intention and action. Based upon this premise, TPB has frequently been deployed to explain the mental process leading up to founding a

24 (Ajzen I., 2001)

business. Studies conducted among students showed a strong, highly significant relationship between self-employment intention and entry into self-employment, suggesting that entry into self-employment is intentional behaviour. Self-employment intention, in turn, is determined by attitude and subjective norms concerning self-employment. Attitudes may be altered in education and training programs. The finding that subjective norm is positively associated with self-employment intentions suggests that we should not only consider the venture idea and the entrepreneur when evaluating or promoting a new venture project. The entrepreneurs' household and significant others should also be taken into consideration. Other explanatory models like Kreuger's adapt this to an entrepreneurial environment wheres the Linan's model evaluated TPB in a multi-country approach.

Krueger's intention model was drawn based on the TPB with some modifications to adapt to an entrepreneurial environment. Accordingly, intentions toward pursuing an opportunity are best predicted by three critical perceptions as (a) personally desirable, (b) supported by social norms, and (c) feasible (feasibility presumably impacted by perceived self-efficacy). This literature has brought in the contextual factors in the environment also working along with the planned behaviour of individual as a deciding element in entrepreneurial intention. Having an entrepreneurial intention means that one is committed to starting a new business[25].

25 (Krueger & Brazeal, 1994)

The Linan's entrepreneurial intention model is based on the theoretical foundation of TPB in congruence with the valuation of environmental cognitive variables considering a multi-country approach. This model well balances the behavioural aspects postulated by TPB, and also the impact of valuations of regional environmental factors in deciding the entrepreneurial intention of students[26]. Thus Linan's model further incorporates the benefits of the Ajzen's intention model as robustness checks using different country samples provide remarkable uniformity in the country samples, considering that the samples have been compiled in highly diverse cultural environments, which has been well assimilated in Linan's model. The findings of the model argue that the evaluations by general society and closer environment of family and friends have a significant impact on behavioural motivators formulated in TPB while deciding the entrepreneurial intention of students. This closer valuation of entrepreneurship seems to exert a substantial influence over personal attitude towards the behaviour. Also social valuation affects perceptions regarding behavioural control (feasibility). Secondly, these effects are different depending on regional differences.

An account of theoretical models explaining entrepreneurial intentions is presented in the table No.2.2

26 (Liñán, Urbano, & Guerrero, 2011)

Table No.2.2 Theoretical Models on Entrepreneurial Intention

Theoretical Model	Formulators	Key Dimensions
1. SEE Model	Shapero & Sokol, 1982	Perceived Feasibility & Perceived Desirability
2. Bird's Model	Bird B., 1988	Intra psychic & Social Organisation
3. TPB Model	Ajzen, 1991	Attitude to Behavior, Subjective Norms & Perceived Behavioral Control
4. Entrepreneurial Potential Model	Krueger & Brazeal, 1994	Personal Desirability, Social Norms, Feasibility
5. Psychologic Economical Model	Davidsson P., 1995	Behavioural Factors & Contextual Factors
6. Linan's EI Model	Lin˜a′n, Urbano, & Guerrero, 2011	Environmental Factors & Behavioural Motivators

The review of theoretical models unveils the relevance of evaluating the individual behavioural factors associated with environmental factors to conclude intentions for entrepreneurship.

Many a times, the students are not able to identify their entrepreneurial intention at an early stage. From a very young age, they would be nurturing the typical ambitions like to be a doctor, engineer, advocate, rocket scientist so on and so forth and being an entrepreneur does not seem very popular unless they are from a family of business. These theories serve as references for those constructs which the mentors or teachers could put to use even at the school level to identify those children who have a unrealized entrepreneurial intention and nurture it early on.

Grolius- the abbreviation of "Grow like us", is an established tech company offering web solutions for schools, tution centres and small business. Surprisingly, none of the team members are older than 15 years old. As part of an initiative to introduce coding and programming basics to school students, a few alumni members who run software business started taking classes at the alma mater. In the end of session assessment, they also included an evaluation of entrepreneurial intention of these kiddos of 5th and 6th standard and the results of 12 students were outstanding. With the help of school teachers, the mentors of the alumni parent company by the name Talrop started giving training in advanced programming and entrepreneurship to these smart and ambitious kids which eventually led to the formation of Grolius, which is a much sought after IT solutions firm among the small business owners in villages of Kerala for its quality offerings at affordable prices and excellent service terms. While the core team of Grolius continue pursuing their innovation and inspiring other kids to grow like them, the mentor company Talrop has assumed their mission to spread the spirit of entrepreneurship as the path to self reliance early on among school students, establishing itself as a startup ecosystem developer in educational institutions.

2.3 Students' Entrepreneurial Intention

Now that we have discussed entrepreneurial intention and its influencing theoretical models from students' perspective, let us understand what exactly is "students' entrepreneurial intention". After the upsurge in student entrepreneurship and the development of theories on this phenomenon, people started to be concerned about what makes students take the entrepreneurial plunge. Segragating students' entrepreneurial intention comes with its own challenges.

Students whose behaviour has not effectively generated any action thus are rendering it impossible to measure in terms of whether or not they have set up a company. In contrast to the market-driven traditional entrepreneurs, the most common driver among young entrepreneurs is having a great business idea that addresses a perceived gap in the market. However, these intentions varied concerning their level of creativity, access to start-up capital, family background, business experience, self-efficacy, the influence of business-minded friends, exposure to entrepreneurial learning, risk propensity, age, course studied and ethnicity.

It was also found that entrepreneurial intentions increased with increase in age. Existence of a strong entrepreneurial intention would make individuals crave for an entrepreneurial pursuit even while enjoying an employed career which makes many students leave their campus placements after a couple of years and build their startup. This is characteristic of the effectual model which is seen among most of the student entrepreneurs who begin with given means and seek to create new ends using non-predictive strategies.

The psychological school argues that people plan their entrepreneurial intention according to their traits and individual dispositions. The sociological school focuses on contextual factors like family and environmental dynamics and suggests that early childhood influences affect career decision. Apart from friends and family, the social norm is reflected in the institutional environment in which the individual operates. However, policy interventions can help only if explicit factors like presence of entrepreneurial management competencies are also analysed as a subject factor of students entrepreneurial intention which would guide them to be realistic with their aspirations. Based on the extensive review of the literature and intensive research among students, an influence factors of students' entrepreneurial intention is presented below.

Contextual Environment: As a student, the first element of consideration in whatever decision he makes is centred around his closer environment comprising family, friends and significant others. The influence of these environmental factors depending on the individual bonding shared can have very strong influence on forming entrepreneurial intentions. However, regional variations and relative differences in valuations by environmental factors can substantially affect the entrepreneurial intention. The underlying factors of general environment carried on through societal values, socio-cultural norms can also have a critical role in the evaluation of entrepreneurial choices. However, the closer environment of the aspiring student has a better influence than the general environment. This influence can be positive or negative based on the closer valuation by the members.

When Aswath Hegde, hailing from a middle class, lost his investment of Rs. 42 Lakhs in his first venture at the age of 22, he was withdrawn and depressed. But his family was not ready to give up on him. His mother lent him Rs. 15000 to give another shot to his entrepreneurial spark. EnviGreen Biotech India, the firm launched by this youngster produces eco-friendly carry bags boasts of an annual turnover of Rs. 30 crore making him a Forbes listed entrepreneur.

Thus, these evaluations can encourage as well as discourage students' perceived control of entrepreneurial behaviour and thereby intention. Moreover, these factors of the closer environment and general environment significantly affect the determination of behavioural motivators of entrepreneurial intentions of students in varying degrees. The contribution of environmental factors may trigger pre-existing behavioural motivators of student entrepreneurs as the same is also taken into consideration while decision making.

- **Behavioural Motivators**: On the lines of Theory of Planned Behavior intentions are assumed to capture the motivational factors that influence behaviour; they are indications of how hard people are willing to try, of how much of an effort they are planning to exert, to perform the behaviour. Over the years, several researchers have empirically tested and confirmed the relevance of this model in explaining the entrepreneurial intention. This will serve as a self assessment for any aspiring entrepreneur to check his own stenghth of entrepreneurial attitude, evaluations by people important to him as well as the levels of behavioural control he can exert on himself.

To be an entrepreneur, one need not be of extremely dynamic personality characteristics. You may not be an attention catcher in the room or every one's super hero, go to person or brilliant problem solver. This would be one reason why successful entrepreneurs are known to be great thinkers in their early life, sometimes even labelled as introverts. If you are outspoken and charismatic, that might help you definitely to a great extent, but what matters more is the strong motivation to execute something which you strongly believes upon.

Elon Musk, the sci-fi entrepreneur has always been vocal about his difficult childhood which made him a behaviorally challenged person during his young days. But he strongly held on to his mission," to strive for greater collective enlightenment" which he has set on for himself as a 14 year old kid. His pattern of self motivation through rigorous knowledge hunt through learning and experimenting continues relentless even being a centibillionaire founding SpaceX, Tesla Inc. Neuralink, OpenAI and many other to his credit.

- **Entrepreneurial Management Competencies**: Its not just starting up, but standing up and scaling up is necessary to survive. This is where it is absolutely essential to know one's competency to manage the dream venture to a commercial success matters. Entrepreneurial management competency refers to the essential management competencies every aspiring entrepreneur must possess or imbibe to transform the venture idea to a marketable business with profit generation abilities. The certain specific set of characteristics referred to as competencies are organised around the individual's underlying entrepreneurial intent and their accurate identification determines the predictive effectiveness of the intention. Earlier, this was considered as a post-development concept, though ample emphasis is given nowadays due to focus on reducing the startup mortality by enabling them to scaleup, which calls for preassessment of these competencies. The significance of specific entrepreneurial management competencies as a determinant of entrepreneurial intention has also slowly been up-and-coming though quite fragmented.

The management competencies that can be brought to bear at this stage, as in other stages of development, may differ enormously. Some would-be entrepreneurs may have formal management education such as an MBA. Others may have many years of experience in the private and/or public sectors. Yet others may be virtually innocent of any such expertise and experience, bringing with them only ideas, or a fledgeling invention, and enthusiasm. All will develop their management skills --though, clearly, to vastly varying degrees-- through learning by doing. As the various propositions and theoretical explanations of management competencies for entrepreneurship are drawn from different contexts, generalisation concerning the knowledge and skillsets is hard to fix upon. However, an all-encompassing broad classification would be on two factors namely, regulatory compliance and managerial abilities.

The factor, regulatory compliance loads on to the reported level of knowledge and skill on tax and government regulations, shareholders' rights and obligations, liabilities and support requirements in marketing. The second factor which measured general proficiency in management like business plan development, marketing and production process. As these items reported the abilities for the overall management of the business, this factor was labelled, managerial abilities. Rather than aiming at functional management competencies at the early stage, it would be better to concentrate on these entrepreneurial management competencies which can be measured across all categories of students.

A realistic assessment of the entrepreneurial intention of students need a higher validation on several aspects to let alone business idea. Should the policy initiatives reach its ambitious goals, a pragmatic and realistic approach is needed to convert a reasonable percentage of students' startup ideas to revenue-generating business entities. This needs to start from grass root level by way of identifying those individual students with strong entrepreneurial spark and flair, precisely characterising their entrepreneurial intention to survive the risks of venture creation. Going by the conventional wisdom that the weak fall, predicting performance based on strength of intention is pertinent to raise entrepreneurs who can productively contribute to the business aspirations of the nation. However, ascertaining the influencers of students' entrepreneurial intention and disseminating them would be helpful to inculcate an aspiration among those students with otherwise not so strong entrepreneurial intention, by way of academic interventions creating an encouraging supporting framework. Understanding how well the emerging environmental support could influence and instil motivators of entrepreneurial intention can give a new boost to the designers of policy formulations and programmes in this regard. Recognising relevant management competencies and framing system to inculcate them among student entrepreneurs could strengthen their startup intention.

Do you have that Spark in you?

Read the following statements carefully and indicate your level of agreement with the following statements about the entrepreneurial activity from 1 (total disagreement) to 5 (total agreement).

1. Starting a firm and keeping it viable would be easy for me.
2. A career as an entrepreneur is totally unattractive to me.
3. My friends would approve of my decision to start a business.
4. I am ready to be an entrepreneur.
5. I believe I would be completely unable to start a business.
6. I will make every effort to start and run my own business.
7. I am able to control the creation process of a new business.
8. My immediate family would approve of my decision to start a business.
9. I have serious doubts about ever starting my own business.
10. If I had the opportunity and resources, I would love to start a business.
11. My colleagues would approve of my decision to start a business.

12. I am determined to create a business venture in the future.
13. Among various options, I would rather be anything but an entrepreneur.
14. If I tried to start business, I would have a high chance of being successful.

** This is an adaptation of Linan's EIQ V.3 scale*

If your score is above 56, keep the spirits up and kindle the spark to a start-up.

If your score falls within 38 to 56, you have moderate intention and entrepreneurship is not your first option.

If your score is less than 38, your intention is very feeble to pursue entrepreneurship.

In a validation exercise conducted among 500 students, it was found that around 20% scored high, 46% moderate while 34% scored to have very low intention to pursue entrepreneurship.

Chapter 3

Enablers of Student Entrepreneurship

"We cannot always build the future for our youth, but we can build our youth for the future"

– Franklin D. Roosevelt

Byjus App- An young tutor's unicorn business

Exam preparation using smartphones was a real irony as exam times used to be the strictly forbidden time for television or any gadgets for that matter. But, Byju's App developed by Byju Raveendran changed it as parents readily started handing over the smartphone or other devices to kids for their video-based visualised concept learning and preparation. Tutoring came naturally to Byju who was the son of two teachers and his lucid explanation of concepts was sought by many of his friends from a very young age itself. The turnaround happened in 2008 after he scored 100 percentile for the Common Admission Test (CAT)for management education in India, which he casually attempted as he was helping some of his friends who were in CAT preparation during his vacation. Just to ensure, he attempted the tough entrance exam next year too and repeated his 100 percentile. Rather than joining any Tier 1 institution, he decided to share his teaching content as a video for higher reach and it helped many. In 2011, Byju Raveendran established the company Think and Learn, persuaded by his students who passed out of IIMs and wanted to offer their tutor's service to millions through online domains. Thus borne Byjus App, serving personalised educational content to millions and joining the prestigious unicorn club with an estimated worth of $1 billion by the year 2019.

3.1 Student entrepreneurs– The naïve' butterflies

Now that we know how to spot a kid who could be the next poster boy or girl for entrepreneurship, let us move on to the action part. Student entrepreneurs are like the newly emerging butterflies out of the cocoon. Given some patience and time, with their inner strength, they will fly out as beautiful butterflies. This is where the enablers have to contribute and drive this evolution. There is a multitude of reasons why the present generation of students are worth considering to build an entrepreneurial society. Gen Y and Gen Z which they belong to are the ambassadors of the information age, equipped with smartphones and most modern gadgets powered by IoT (Internet of Things). They have wide social circles and shared interest through online networks. Creativity and street smartness of today's students keeps them less intimidated by the uncertainties and more adventurous to take risks. Most of them are rationale and prefer to construct and make a difference in the world rather than being instructed. These naïve yet forthcoming nature of today's student makes him an ideal building block for the entrepreneurial society in the making. Parents, teachers, cousins, friends, policy makers.... grab your robe and be the super power in the student's entrepreneurial path. If you are a student reader, people with great power have greater responsibilities; make use of them for your good!

We are familiar to the story of Google which was backed by the trinity of Stanford faculty members, family and friends who nurtured the famous duo Larry page and Sergey Brin. The pooled finance to buy some servers and rental space in a garage and the moral backing laid the founding pillars to start their entrepreneurial space. Later when they received their first investment cheque from Anty Bechtolsheim, the cofounder of Sun Microsystems, they did not have a bank account or even the courage to correct the venture name misspelled as "Google" in the cheque instead of "Googol" which they had planned. Eventually they opened a bank account with the misspelled name itself to deposit the cheque and an era of SEO was borne.

The components of the physical and social environment of the student need to address the significance of promoting entrepreneurial spark of students, through their business start-ups by converting job seekers to job creators. It is imperative for any economy with an aim for self-sustaining progressive development to support and reinforce the entrepreneurial intention of the youngsters, to contain the employment prospects of its growing population. The direct causal relationship between the students' business orientations and regional economic growth is a well-established fact. The changing demographic profile in many countries is also leading to a significant increase in young people as a percentage of the total population. As the formal sector of employment in many countries experience stagnant or sluggish growth, it is improbable that this sector will be able to offer employment opportunities to the increasing number of young people looking for employment. Unless alternative employment options are encouraged, the number of unemployed, underemployed youths and youth in vulnerable employment will continue to increase. This is more than enough reason to empower youth entrepreneurship, as a supplementary way of allowing the youth into the labour market and promoting job creation.

With students as focal point of tomorrow's entrepreneurial economy, the enabling role of every stakeholder in nurturing the entrepreneurial intention need to be identified and put into action. In addition to the student fraternity and policy makers, society at large has realized the ever increasing scope of students turning entrepreneurs and appreciate the grander milieu for economic development. The multiple enablers that can directly impact students and encourage their start up ambitions are presented below for the reader to identify his relative importance in the making of an entrepreneur or many.

Government

The current measures adopted by the government centres around encouraging student entrepreneurship through creation of a supportive ecosystem. This could be a springboard for budding entrepreneurs since it includes multiple schemes for handholding spread across incubation, acceleration, infrastructure, tax exemptions, legal support, intellectual property registration, preferences in govt. tenders, academia, collaborations, mentoring and easy exit options, tax savings for investors, startup fests etc.. Creating a positive vibe around student entrepreneurship by government led promotion can create a lot of mileage.

Kerala, the southernmost state of India is known for its high literacy rates and green rich natural beauty. For years, Kerala has been considered as a consumer state with nothing to boast of in enterprise sector. Though importance of education is a prime mover in the state, thanks to the "white-collar hypothesis," there was a steady exodus to Middle East and US in search of greener pastures adding to brain drain. The Student Startup Policy which was rolled out by the government in 2015 aiming to reverse this brain drain had an exceptional impact since it focused on identifying entrepreneurs from campus itself. The unprecedented grace mark allowance and attendance waivers for students pursuing entrepreneurship was later taken as a model by other states too. Over a period of time, the state has placed itself in the top ranks with respect to student entrepreneurial ecosystem in India.

The starting point of the operational support system mostly starts with the student submitting a project idea to the government agencies for entrepreneurial development. The government intervention with regard to entrepreneurial ecosystem development should cover a broader scope. A structured and scientific entrepreneurial intention assessment system to screen the beneficiaries of the policy rather than the idea based allotment can ensure nurturing the right prospects to startup and scaleup. Appreciating the fact that students are most affected by the evaluation of the closer environment, the government should intervene with necessary activities to sensitise the members of family, educational institutions as well as society in a positive manner towards business as a promising prospective career option for the students. As the emerging environmental factors are strongly contributing to the behavioural motivators of entrepreneurial intention among students the policy makers may develop comprehensive framework incorporating students, academics and parents which could compliment the mentoring and incubation system. Directives with regard to inclusion of entrepreneurship as a curricular subject in the syllabus right from the school level and practical vocational option in college level can be made mandatory. Essential steps must be adopted to reduce the associated red-tapism when it comes to promising entrepreneurial ideas. Specialised courses and institutions for nurturing the entrepreneurship and entrepreneurial management competencies should be set up by the government.

Family and Significant Others

Young or old, entrepreneur or otherwise, we all often anchor for anything and everything with our family and other close ones. Similiarly, aspiring young entrepreneurs also seek emotional support, financial support as well as operational support from family and significant others and they have a pivotal role to play in the way ahead. Since entrepreneurial intention of students is a factor of their pre-existing behavioural motivators, students should be motivated right from a young age by the members of the family and society to be self –dependent.

It was a dining table discussion between Mehal and her father on milk adulteration which led to her organic dairy startup. Her father Vivek, with his rich entrepreneurial experience was sure that after a few such complaints and discussions, his daughter will come up with a solution to curb the adulterated milk consumption and she did it. When Mehal's research threw her the insight that around 70% of milk and milk products in the country did not meet FSSAI (Food Safety and Standards Authority of India) norms, she decided to take bull by its horns. Before her initial spirits set down, Vivek took it to the next level by bootstrapping the organic milk farm," Happy Milk", with a starting customer base of 3000 daily customers, all when Mehal was just 22 years old.

The first investors in most of the student business are their parents or family members as the seed capital to startup would have been given by them. This helps the newbie to set up the initial setup with a better mental frame as family funding is a reflection of family support itself. By and large startup investors turn to the family itself for their operational support also like manpower and expertise especially in the early stages until they can afford external staffing. This kind of early interventions can positively influence the students to consider entrepreneurship as a viable option for employment as they grow up and may actively pursue their entrepreneurial intentions. There should be profuse encouragement from family and society for students to try their hands on business and get themselves aware about and avail the policy benefits provided by government in this regard.

Educational Institutions

"What is your ambition?", this is a regular question which school students often get to answer. This question is an indicator of the critical role educational institutions play in the goal setting. As attitude shaping takes time, right from the school level itself efforts are needed to instil a positive attitude towards entrepreneurship too along with other career options. Even if one student changes his attitude towards self-employment, it can create a cascading effect throughout the society where he lives by word of mouth. Since general environment can affect the entrepreneurial intention of students at a larger dimension, the educational institutions have a bigger role in identifying and nurturing students with strong entrepreneurial intention.

Naveen Tiwari, the studious boy joined for his PhD programme at Harvard with similar aspiration as many of his family members; to take up a teaching role in an IIT. But what he later consider as the "pivotal years" of his life in the campus, enabled him to go beyond the restrictive thinking of a middle class Indian boy and motivating him to trust his capabilities and think big. After dabbling in a few startup plans eventually to set up the unicorn Inmobi, he had a very special person joining him onboard-his teacher and mentor Tarun Khanna. Tarun Khanna is renowned as a passionate professor in entrepreneurship cofounding and nurturing many of his students's startup ventures around the world.

Along with academic preparation for getting placement, students should be encouraged to consider entrepreneurship as a viable employment option. Modifying the academic grading system with ample credit for entrepreneurial activities could boost the student aspirations. Most of the Indian states give credit to the entrepreneurial aptitude of students by providing grace marks and attendance waivers. Necessary intervention which could help students to inculcate and build on the specific entrepreneurial management competencies can be done by academics to enhance the intention of students. Nevertheless, inculcating even the basic managerial competencies through start-up mentoring could impact the entrepreneurial intentions. From the graduate level and above, specialised screening methods can be put to use for early identification and nurturing of students with entrepreneurial potential at the time of joining and induction. Entrepreneurial education should be provided as a part of curriculum itself. Maximising the entrepreneurial exposures through interactions with entrepreneurs, facility visits, attending startup events, awareness sessions etc. can create a positive attitude towards entrepreneurship among students. Incorporating the government policies on entrepreneurship through specialised cell activities with monitoring and governance can develop an entrepreneurial culture within the educational institution.

Students

Considering the fact that entrepreneurial intention is a measurable variable, students could make a realistic self-assessment of the same before venturing into business. Instead of the common practice of converting a meritorious academic project to the business plan, they should focus on developing need based solutions through market research. Once they identify the genuine entrepreneurial intention and decide entrepreneurial career, effort must be taken to imbibe and assimilate the necessary entrepreneurial management competencies to sustain the venture. Rather than diving into startup wooed by stories of glory alone, their aspiration should be weighed based on the social valuations of failed predecessors also. Socialisation which will help in strengthening entrepreneurial identities should be cherished. Setting up realistic dreams through active learning from accessible role models on how to handle failures and uncertainties can transform the student business ideas to scalable entrepreneurial ventures.

My Support System

Do you want to know how well others support your entrepreneurial aspirations? Assessing the general environment support for entrepreneurship is very important to know the viability of starting a business.

Following is a set of statements which would help you to assess the general ecosystem around you to support your entrepreneurial aspiration. Carefully read the statements and mark your agreement as 1(total disagreement) to 5 (total agreement).

1. My immediate family, values entrepreneurial activity above other activities.
2. The culture in my region is highly favorable towards entrepreneurial activity.
3. The entrepreneur's role in economy is generally undervalued in my region.
4. My friends value entrepreneurial activities and careers.
5. Most people around me consider it unacceptable to be an entrepreneur.
6. In my region, entrepreneurial activity is considered to be worthwhile, despite risks.
7. My classmates value entrepreneurial activity above other activities and careers.
8. It is commonly thought that entrepreneurs take advantage of others.

Find your total score and compare it with the standards below.

- *If the score is more than 32, hurray!!!! You have an awesome support system*
- *If the score is in the range of 5-32, they are not yet convinced about entrepreneurship as an option for you!*
- *If the score is less than 5, it will be very difficult to get any support from around!*

In a validation exercise conducted among 500 students, it was found that around 26% scored high, 40% moderate while 34% scored to have very low support from their general environment.

Chapter 4

Handling Success and Failures

"Success is not final, failure is not fatal: it is the courage to continue that counts."

– Winston Churchill

Softronics, the first venture by the legend N.R.Narayana Murthy failed miserably within a short period of hardly a year and a half. He went back to a corporate job determined to do a clinical analysis of his failure. In his own words," 'look, I fell down, therefore I dusted my knee, got up and then I said look I learnt this lesson from this failure and I will go, take up a corporate job, understand what the global markets are and start my own venture' (Murthy 2013). In 1981 with a borrowed capital of Rs.10000 from his wife, co-founded Infosys, which became the global leader in digial services and consulting. Renowned as the Father of Indian IT Sector, Narayana Murthy has pioneered not just the outsorcing industry, but fuelled an economy of first generation entreprenurship in India.

Thousands of literature are available on multiple tips for achieving success in entrepreneurship. Many a times students who venture out into business, would be keen to devour any advice as long as it aids him in his road to business. Those with a very strong intention to succeed will not leave any stone unturned in their path. They get exhilarated as well as emotional in every single milestone achievement. It is equally important that the student should be equipped to celebrate the inevitable failures in the uncertain path of entrepreneurship as opportunities for learning and improving themselves in the process. This chapter is focusing on certain aspects which the newly bred entrepreneurs and ecosystem partners need to thrust upon to ensure a balanced take on success and failures in student business.

4.1 Ideas can be innovations or idiosyncrasies

Students often start their entrepreneurial dreams when they have a knock out idea for a product or service. Their confidence gets boosted up if they get appreciated for their idea by anyone in their social circles and devote themselves to developing a business around it without analyzing the practicalities. The members in the entrepreneurial support system need to help the students to validate the potential of their ideas concerning the pros and cons of realistic entrepreneurship. Those ideas which could be converted to commercial innovation should be filtered out and channeled through proper support system and mentoring to bloom and develop. The others should be encouraged to fail fast rather than progressing ahead as mere idiosyncrasies for the eventual failure. Even if the idea seems to be of no good for present or future opportunities and economic prospects, but the student is genuinely intended to pursue entrepreneurship with remarkable competencies and behavior, he or she should be encouraged with ample moral support to be self-motivated enough to consider working on other innovations.

Advice Monkey, the job-board website business started by the 16 year old Niel Patel consistently ranked on Google for job and career terms. An investment of around 1 million dollar was spent in development, generating more than 100,000 monthly visitors, but not sufficient customers since the product failed to offer what customers wanted. With lessons well learnt early in the startup journey, Niel Patel could later build wildly successful ventures like Kissmetrics, Crazyegg etc. in future.

4.2 Hope for the best, be prepared for the worst

This age-old idiom is so true when it comes to entrepreneurship, which is driven by ultimate optimism but realistic preparation to face adversities that may arise out of underlying uncertainties. Students who are aiming to tread into the path of self-employment need to be loaded with hope, positivity and ample readiness to face disastrous situations that can turn their dream world upside down. While motivating self and others about the possibilities and potentials of success in entrepreneurship, a measured outlook based on the assessment of pitfalls and unavoidable risk should also be known to the student who is venturing into the unpredictable terrain. Seasoned entrepreneurs and experience role models can help the newbie in business in this regard by sharing life stories as well as offering active mentoring.

Slurrp Farm, the organic baby food startup brand founded by two mums was nearing a quick breakeven, as the pandemic Covid-19 loomed the world. The two entrepreneurs, Meghana Narayan and Shauravi Malik kept a close watch on the pandemic defense measures adopted by other countries which were worse hit than India as they plunged into a race for a radical overhaul of the business in warfooting. They were able to takeoff on their new marketing strategy just three days before India went to lockdown. They were equipped to diversify forseeing the emerging lockdown consumption trends. Slurrp Farm not only survived Covid-19, but also doubled their revenues with the new business model and a huge market creation.

4.3 Rational decisions than emotional

Dealing with success as well as failures with a more rational approach than emotional will lead to better decisions in the future course of action. Proper evaluation to identify and segregate the factors which led to success or failure will make the student conditioned to take success and failure with equal ease as learning. Entrepreneurship is never a sprint, but a marathon wherein the naive evolves as a well-rounded business person staying perseverant in the learning curve. Scientific tools which can assess the emotional threshold of the would-be entrepreneur can unveil the unknown behavioral strengths as well as weakness so that the person can be in a better position to understand, predict as well as control their emotions and channel it towards strengthening rational take on success and failure.

Even as an engineering student, Anisha Dhar was always aware of her passion for doing something in foodspace was roasting slowly and steadily within her. As she met a likeminded colleague after her placement in a consulting job, she decided to make the plunge with her food tech startup, Eatanomist, to serve healthy gourmet meals to office desks. They did thorough research and validation of the niche they have found successful enough to secure seed investement, though the real market experience was difficult after launch. Anisha Dhar closed down her startup within three years of operation and took up a corporate job.

4.4 Be honest to self

Young entrepreneurs tend to get driven by the vanity metrics they plot for themselves to emulate their role models. Even though it is considered as an inspiration to set goals and milestones, it must also be an authentic reflection of potential strengths and weakness which will enable the student to stay true to self and convince others involved in the process with honesty and genuineness. Feeling empowered by false and unrealistic components will eventually backfire as these may lead to false promises and lost trust. Getting ecstatic on getting the deals signed is quite normal and definitely, moments which needs to be celebrated but the process gets completed only after ensuring that the deal was converted to a value-added delivery to the people involved.

Jim Triandiflou landed himself in the founder's dilemema as he realized he will have to leave the management control on his startup to the venture capitalist if he wants the much needed funding for his firm's growth. After much soul searching he decided to sell the equity to the venture capitalist. He gave up board control, but managed to see his startup Ockham technologies, which was more like his baby, grow up manifold times in value with the newly gained resources.On the other hand, John Gabbert, the founder of Room & Board, has consistently rejected offers for funding since he wants to live with his own choices.

4.5 Deferred gratification

Most of the times, entreprenurship is all about deferred gratification. Courage and perseverance to resiliently sail through the journey is absolutely essential. Sacrifice and commitment with the hope for a better tomorrow is the key to the fortune. The ability to spot the symptoms of failure early and take deviations can save the entrepreneurship from a bad wreck. Trustworthy social circle who can guide the novice businessman in his blind spots should be closely bound in. It could also save the entrepreneur from getting overly attached to the idea.

Evernote, the Silicon valley startup which is popular among students for its cloud based abiliy to help them with their class notes was at the brimof its crash within years of its stratospheric rise and manifold expansions. As naysayers reported it as the soon to be dead unicorn, the Evernote team was preparing for a difficult turnaround. They garnered courage and discipline to make some tough calls with respect to all elements of their startup, shelving every leisure point until they could finally achieve positive cashflows.

4.6 Attempt a resilience measurement

Resilience is the secret weapon of any entrepreneur to fight through adversities. It is always advisable to self assess the resilience power so that a realistic assessment could be made. This will also help the student business owner to be very realistic about his strengths which could be strongly held on to as well as flaws which needed to be sorted out gauging the uncertain diaspora of entrepreneurship he is venturing into.

When Kaito started his dream startup, Community Coders from his university and won a few pitching competitions, he could visualise his sprawling offices across the country with the creative logo he had designed.Spotting his enterprising nature, the university provided him all opportunities, funding and internship credits. However, his business model stated showing cracks within a few months of operation in the real market due to insufficient product-market fit and lack of knowledge to fix it in the go after establishing, eventually compelling Kaito to shut his dream company, may be for a better comeback later.

Would you like to know how resilient you are?

Here is an adaptation of self assessment tool to check your resilience power, the Connor-Davidson Resilience Scale (CD-RISC-25).

The following represent the items for the 25-item Connor-Davidson Resilience Scale . Rate your agreement in a scale of 5 ranging from not true at all or zero, to true nearly all of the time or four.

1. I am able to adapt when changes occur.
2. I have one close and secure relationship.
3. Sometimes fate or God helps me.
4. I can deal with whatever comes my way.
5. Past successes give me confidence.
6. I try to see the humorous side of things when I am faced with problems.
7. Having to cope with stress can make me stronger.
8. I tend to bounce back after illness, injury or other hardships.
9. I believe most things happen for a reason.
10. I make my best effort, no matter what.
11. I believe I can achieve my goals, even if there are obstacles.
12. Even when hopeless, I do not give up.
13. In times of stress, I know where to find help.
14. Under pressure, I stay focused and think clearly.
15. I prefer to take the lead in problem-solving.
16. I am not easily discouraged by failure.
17. I think of myself as a strong person when dealing with life's challenges and difficulties.
18. I make unpopular or difficult decisions.
19. I am able to handle unpleasant or painful feelings like sadness, fear, and anger.

20. I have to act on a hunch.
21. I have a strong sense of purpose in life.
22. I feel like I am in control.
23. I like challenges.
24. I work to attain goals.
25. I take pride in my achievements.

CD-RISC scale could be used only with permission from the authors available through mail@cd-risc.com.

Chapter 5

No Spark? No worries, Let's try intrapreneurship

I'm innovative, but I don't intent to be an entrepreneur, if you feel like this- read on. Every innovative person is not cut out to be an entrepreneur, but the confidence you have in your innovative ways of doing things will sure enough create a halo around you making you an outstanding person, sometimes a great intrapreneur- an employee with innovative business solutions. Nevertheless, every genius inventor need not make successful businessmen. Some other great innovators prefer not to pursue entrepreneurship for their own reasons, lack of behavioral motivators, limiting contextual elements or complacence even with all competencies in place. Since entrepreneurship is all about value creation through innovation, one can add tremendous value to the organisation he or she serves and the economy at large by being an intrapreneur.

Thomas Alva Edison, the great inventor incorporated The Edison Electric Light Company in 1878 to market his disruptive innovation, the incandescent lights. The company later got acquired to be the part of the mighty General Electricals, popularly known as GE. The name which always resonates with GE is of John Francis Welch, the once junior chemical engineer in GE, who turned around GE as the most competitive company in the world with his inimitable management and enterprising competencies gaining him the nick name "Neutron Jack" and Jack Welch.

Sony Computer Entertainment which markets the iconic PlayStation was the brainchild of an employee, Ken Kutaragi who had been working with Sony Sound Labs. He was trying to develop a game sole for his daughter which had better sound qualities than the one she had been playing with. A few other executives were miffed by his sideline project using company's resources and wanted to sack him. But the CEO of Sony at that time, Norio Ohga realized the potential of his innovative breakthrough idea which could transform the gaming industry and encouraged him which led to the disruptive product Playstation. The founder of the bestselling game console of all time, Ken Kutaragi thus became the founder of Sony's one of the most profitable business division as well.

Intrapreneurship is often considered as entrepreneurship within the safety of a secured job. As entrepreneurship is perceived as risky and speculative, those who prefer the comfort of a steady job could attempt to be an intrapreneur keeping their innovative spirit high by playing the key role in an entrepreneur's turf. It also suits those who always wanted to tread the path of innovation but could not get sufficient contextual support from the environment as well for those who have their creative juices flowing all time though do not dare to catch the bull by its horn single handedly due to low resilience measures.

Progressive enterprises recognized the need for supporting the spirit of intrapreneurship of their employees and provide them with sufficient avenues. Creative challenges, hackathons, ideathons, skunkworks etc. are widely getting popular among organisations big and small. This often leads to creative solutions like Post it which emerged through an innovation challenge at 3M or the like button of Facebook which came up through a hackathon.

So dear student, why wait. buckle up and create value through innovation!

Research Model Premise of the Book

The research model followed in the book for identifying and tapping students' entrepreneurial intention is presented here as an after read.

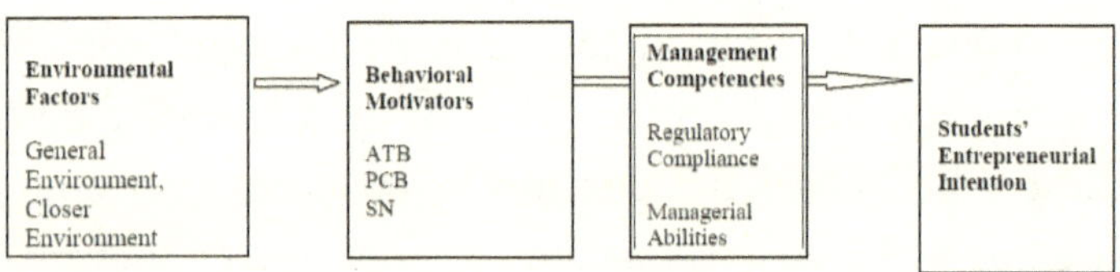

The contextual environment explained in the Chapter two were derived out of the contextual environment in a closer and social level. The behavioral motivators follow the three dimensions of planned behaviour, Attitude to

Behaviour (ATB), Subjective Norms (SN) and Perceived Control of Behavior (PCB). The entrepreneurial management competency of the student focuses on the competency to manage the regulatory compliance as well as the students' general managerial abilities. An assessment of these factors can lead to the evaluationof the students' entrepreneurial intention-or the spark early on.

Bibliography

Ajzen, I. (1991). The Theory of Planned Behavior. In I. Ajzen, Organizational Behavior and Human Decision Processes 50, (pp. 179-211).

Bird, B. (1988). Implementing Entrepreneurial Ideas:The case of intention. *Academy of Management Review Vol 13 No.3*, 142-153.

Franco, M. H. (2010). Students' entrepreneurial intentions: an inter-regional comparison.. *Education + Training, Vol. 52 Iss 4*, 260 - 275.

Kolvereid, L., & Isaksen, E. (2006). New business start-up and subsequent entry into self employment. *Journal of Business Venturing 21*, 866-885.

Krueger, N. F. (2000). Competing Models of Entrepreneurial Intentions. *Journal of Business Venturing 15*, 411–432.

Liñán,. F., & Chen, Y.-W. (2006). Testing the entrepreneurial intention model ona two-country sample. *Documentde Treball núm. 06/7*, 1-28.

Liñán, F., Cohard, J. C., & -Cantuche, J. M. (2011). Factors affecting entrepreneurial intention levels: a role for education. *Int Entrep Manag J*, 195–218.

Mungai, E. M. (2013). *Socio-cultural factors and entrepreneurial intentions of undergraduate students in public universities in Kenya.* Nairobi: School of Business.

Philipp Sieger, U. F. (2014). *Student Entrepreneurship Across the Globe: A Look at Intentions and Activities International Report of the GUESSS Project 2013/2014.* St.Gallen: St.Gallen: Swiss Research Institute of Small Business and Entrepreneurship at the University of St.Gallen (KMU-HSG).

Prabhu, V. P., McGuire, E. S., & Dros, A. (2012). Proactive personality and entrepreneurial intent: Is entrepreneurial self-efficacy mediator or moderator. *International Journal of Entrepreneurial Behavior & Research, Vol. 18 Iss 5*, 559-586.

Rittippant,. N., & Kokchang, W. P. (2011). Measure of Entrepreneurial Intention of Young adults in Thailand. *EPPM*, 20-21.

Valliere, D. (2016). Measuring Regional Variations of Entrepreneurial Intent in India. *The Journal of Entrepreneurship,* 111–128.

Wu, J. (2009). *Entrepreneurial Orientation, Entrepreneurial Intent and New Venture Creation: Test of a Framework in a Chinese Context.* Virginia: Faculty of Virginia Polytechnic Institute.

Author Bio

Dr. Deepa Unnithan PhD, is an Academic, Researcher and Mentor of Student Entrepreneurs and Management students. Her research in student entrepreneurship was published as book chapters, case studies and articles. She has presented several research papers in the focus arca of student entrepreneurship and serves as a reviewer in Emerald Insights and Publons. As a management graduate with UGC-NET and PhD as well as industrial experience in different levels of management cadre in media and banking, she teaches courses on entrepreneurial development for MBA courses and conducts regular workshops on scientific assessment of students' entrepreneurial intention and development to promote campus entrepreneurial culture and actively mentors startups from the campus to viable business models.

Dr. Hareesh N Ramanathan is a passionate academician and an entrepreneur mentor with around twenty years of professional experience. He is educated in the field of management and secured a doctoral degree as well in management. He has been instrumental in creating new entrepreneurs in varied domains. He has designed a curriculum at the graduate level to identify and nurture entrepreneurs in the early stage and to groom them along with their academic pursuits. He is an IBM certified analyst and hence orienting entrepreneurs and students to have an analytical acumen to understand the business problems in a much-refined way. He has taken entrepreneurship consultancies in the area of tourism, hospitality, baking, information technology, hardware, hotel and restaurants. He has taught entrepreneurship in foreign universities and is constantly associated with entrepreneurship research.

www.ingramcontent.com/pod-product-compliance
Lightning Source LLC
La Vergne TN
LVHW091222150826
845673LV00003B/975

* 9 7 9 8 8 8 6 2 9 9 3 8 0 *